101 FAVORITE WILD RICE RECIPES

Dr. Duane R. Lund

Distributed by
Adventure Publications, Inc.
820 Cleveland St. S.
Cambridge, MN 55008

Printed in the United States of America
1st Printing, 1983
2nd Printing, 1983
3rd Printing, 1984
4th Printing, 1985
5th Printing, 1987
6th Printing, 1988
7th Printing, 1989
8th Printing, 1993
9th Printing, 1998
10th Printing, 1999
11th Printing, 2001
12th Printing, 2003
13th Printing 2007
14th Printing 2010

ISBN-13: 978-0-934860-24-6
ISBN-10: 0-934860-24-6

Dedication:

*To the Truman Sandland family,
pioneers in the cultivation of wild rice.*

TABLE OF CONTENTS

Page No.

I   INTRODUCTION 9

II   SERVING TIPS 15

III   BASIC PREPARATION RECIPES 17
Method #**1** 17
Method #**2** 18
Method #**3** 18
Method #**4** 18
Method #**5** 18

IV   SIDE DISH RECIPES 19
6 Wild Rice with Mushrooms 19
7 Wild Rice with Cream of Mushroom Soup 19
8 Nutty Rice 20
9 Seasoned Rice in a Skillet 20
10 Bacon Flavored Wild Rice 21
11 Spicy Wild Rice with Mushrooms 21
12 Baked Wild Rice with Olives and Cheese 22
13 Onion Soup Mix - Wild Rice Side Dish 22

V   WILD RICE WITH VEGETABLES 23
14 Wild Rice and Zucchini 23
15 Wild Rice and Broccoli 23
Stuffing Recipes for Baked Peppers, Squash, or Tomatoes
16 Orange Flavored Stuffing 24
17 Broccoli Stuffing 25
18 Spanish Stuffing 25
19 Stove Top Wild Rice and Garden Vegetables 26
20 Pepper Boats with Wild Rice Stuffing 26
21 Wild Rice with Asparagus 27
22 Wild Rice with Spinach 27
23 Oriental Vegetables with Wild Rice 28

**VI   SOUPS, BROTHS, STEWS, AND
        MULLIGANS** 31
24 Vegetable Beef Soup with Wild Rice 31
25 Scotch Broth with Venison 31
26 Wash Day Soup 32
27 Pheasant - Rice Soup 32
28 Small Game Mulligan 33
29 Quick Big Game Stew 33
30 Wild Rice and Canned Soups 33
31 Wild Rice and Packaged Soups 34

32 "Bargain" Wild Rice with Soups or Stews 34
33 Wild Rice as a Substitute 34
34 Creamy Mushroom Wild Rice Soup 34
35 Quick Vegetable Stew. 35

VII WILD RICE WITH BIG GAME OR DOMESTIC MEATS 37
36 Wild Rice with Ham Chunks (Casserole) 37
37 Cabbage Rolls with Wild Rice 37
38 Chop Suey Casserole 38
39 Baked Steak with Wild Rice and Mushrooms 38
40 Ham Loaf 39
41 Porcupine Meat Balls with Sweet and Sour Sauce 39
42 Baked Pork Chops 40
43 Ham and Turkey Rolls 40
44 Meatloaf with Wild Rice 41
45 Swiss Baked Steak with Wild Rice 41
46 South Seas Stuffed Steak Rolls 42
47 Wild Rice and Sirloin 42
48 Venison and Wild Rice Hash 43
49 Wild Rice and Hamburger Hotdish 43
50 Wild Rice - Venison Sausage Casserole 44
51 Venison Stroganoff. 44
52 Spicy Rice Roll-up with Hamburger 45
53 Rabbit Stew with Wild Rice Dumplings 46

VIII WILD RICE WITH DUCKS, UPLAND GAME, AND DOMESTIC BIRDS 47
54 Wild Rice with Partridge 47
55 Wild Rice with Duck Casserole 48
56 Wild Rice, Mushrooms, and Turkey Leftovers 48
57 Pheasant, Partidge or Mallard Wild Rice Hotdish 49
58 Half Ducks on a Bed of Rice 49
59 Gourmet Roast Duck with Wild Rice Stuffing and
Honey Glaze 50
60 Pheasant breasts with Wild Rice 51
61 Turkey Roll-ups 52
62 Duck Breasts with Wild Rice and Onion Soup Mix 53
63 Chicken-stuffed Pepper Boats. 53

Wild Rice Dressing Recipes
64 Sausage Stuffing 53
65 Nutty Stuffing 54
66 Bacon Stuffing 54
67 Seasoney Stuffing 55
68 Dinner in a Skillet 55

IX WILD RICE AND SEA FOODS 57
69 Wild Rice and Shrimp 57
70 Fish Loaf. 57
71 Wild Rice with Shrimp and Sweet and Sour Sauce 58

72 Wild Rice with King Crab 59
73 Wild Rice Salmon Loaf 59
74 Wild Rice and Baked Oysters .60
75 Oyster Dressing 60
76 Lemon Rubbed and Wine-basted Baked Fish with
    Wild Rice Dressing 61
77 Wild Rice and Baked Snapping Turtle 61

X   **WILD RICE IN BAKED GOODS** 63
78 Wild Rice Bread 63
79 Blueberry and Wild Rice Muffins 64
80 Wild Rice and Red River Cereal Bread 64
81 Baking Powder Biscuits 65
82 Wild Rice Dumplings 65
83 Miscellaneous Baking Recipes .65

XI   **SALADS** 67
84 Seafood Salad 67
85 Glorified Rice 67
86 Garden Salad 68
87 Chicken Salad 68
88 Stuffed Tomato Salad 68
89 Three Bean Salad 69

XII **DESSERTS** 71
90 Rice Pudding 71
91 Wild Rice with Granola 71
92 Wild Rice with Fruit 71
93 Wild Rice and Wild Berries 72
94 Wild Rice Custard 72

XIII **BREAKFASTS** 73
95 Wild Rice as a Hot Cereal 73
Pancakes and Waffles
96 With Cooked Wild Rice 73
97 With Wild Rice Flour 73
98 From Scratch 74

XIV **HORS D' OEUVRES** 75
99 Popped Wild Rice 75
100 Mini-Porcupines 75
101 Wild Rice and Chicken Liver Canopés 76

I INTRODUCTION

WILD RICE is one of the most exotic and romantic of all foods.

It is forever entwined in the history of the American Indian. For centuries, wild rice made the difference between life and death for these Native Americans during countless long, cold winters. Many a battle was fought between the Chippewa and the Sioux for the right to harvest the water-supported grain.

Mallards, teal, pintails, widgeon, and other puddle ducks still gorge themselves on wild rice each fall as they prepare for the long flight south, or merely grow plump in preparation for the hunter's table.

Wild rice is among the most delicious—and yet nutritious—of all foods. It has been a gourmet favorite ever since white man was first introduced to its nutty flavor by the Indian in the 17th century. All over the United States, Canada, and even Europe, wild rice dishes provide the finishing touch to the banquet table. Whenever and wherever served, it is associated with luxurious cuisine.

When we think of wild rice, we dream of stuffed roast duck— of rich side dishes well laced with mushrooms—of creamy casseroles—of pheasant under glass—of slow baked northern pike or salmon.

Minnesota, Ontario, and parts of northern Wisconsin and Michigan have a natural monopoly on wild rice. Small quantities are grown in California and some other parts of Canada, but the amount is relatively insignificant. Wild rice was a very important part of the Indians' diet on this part of the continent and was one of the few foods that could be easily and indefinitely stored. However, it is not a true rice. In fact, the first French explorers more correctly described the grain as "wild oats". Actually, it is a unique food only remotely related to any other.

Early white men were nearly as dependent on wild rice for survival as were the Indians. The historic massacre of twenty French soldier-voyageurs and Father Alneau on Lake of the Woods in 1734 may never have happened if the wild rice crop had not been devastated by high water, making it necessary for nearly half the contingent at Fort St. Charles to start back East before winter set in. They were attacked by the Sioux as they made camp on an island; all were killed.[1]

The commercial growers of today use artificial paddies, weed and water control and have adapted conventional farm machinery to make a profitable operation possible. The University of Minnesota is cooperating with the farmer in developing new strains which are more resistant to wind and hail and which have non-shattering heads, which means the grain may be harvested at one time, by machine, in a single operation. The kernels of rice in the same head of natural varieties ripen at different times over several days so that they are not all ripe for harvest at the same time. This is why a rice bed may be harvested again and again over a couple of weeks as the new kernels ripen. This is also the reason the law requires the use of canoes or narrow boats so that the rice is not beaten down and wasted, but may be worked several times. Surprisingly, there has been no improvement in the harvesting of the non-domestic rice over the method used by the Indians down through the centuries. The stalks are bent over the boat and the ripe kernels are beaten from the heads into the boat—usually with stout sticks. Air boats with catcher nets on either side have been used on an experimental basis, but this permits only a single run through the rice bed and most of it goes to waste.

There was also the Indian custom of tying some of the rice into bundles just before it ripened, leaving the plants to continue their growth. These were then harvested as a bundle and this rice had a different flavor and was considered a special delicacy.

As we stated earlier, for family purposes the Indian method has not been improved. The harvested rice was parched over or near heat, stirring slowly so that it would not burn. Once the kernels were loosened from the husks, the rice was removed from the heat and pounded. Indians used a large wooden container as a mortar and a pointed post as a pestle. Once the separation was complete, the rice was winnowed by throwing it in the air over a sheet of birchbark or a blanket on a windy day. The chaff blew away. As a final step, the last remnants of husks

---

[1]More Lake of the Woods history may be found in another book by this author entitled *"Lake of the Woods, Yesterday and Today,"* Nordell Graphics, Staples, MN 56479.

The stalks are bent over the boat and the ripe kernels are beaten from the head with a stout stick.

were removed by trampling with clean moccasins. If there were large quantities of rice, the Indians rested on their hands or elbows on poles secured to either side of a large tree. Once again the rice was winnowed; this time the chaff was saved and cooked like wild rice. The grain could be stored in a cool, dry place—indefinitely.

It is unfortunate that most people today think of wild rice as an expensive food. If you have not cooked with wild rice, it will surprise you how many dishes and complete meals can be made

The harvested rice is parched over or near heat, stirring regularly so the kernels will not burn.

Once the kernels are loosened from the husks, the rice is removed from the heat and pounded.

Courtesy Minnesota Historical Society

from a single pound. A myth also prevails that wild rice is difficult to prepare. Not true! It is actually quite hard to spoil wild rice. Just give it a try. In fact, dear reader, this book is dedicated to you; it is guaranteed to help convince both family and friends that you are truly a gourmet chef!

Wild rice will turn the most ordinary of meals into a banquet.

Modern day harvesting of wild rice on the Truman Sandland farm near Clearbrook, Minnesota, after the paddies have been drained.

II
SERVING TIPS

1. Always wash the rice thoroughly before cooking. If you use a sieve or colander, run faucet water through the rice until it runs clear a few minutes.

2. The more uncooked rice is washed, the milder the flavor.

3. If rice is to be cooked further as a part of another recipe, it is better that it be a little under-cooked.

4. In addition to salt, you may wish to add a little pepper and/or other spices such as oregano, parsley flakes, marjoram, onion salt, etc.

5. The addition of butter or margarine to the cooked rice seems to keep it firm.

6. Wild rice can usually be substituted for white or brown rices.

7. Wild rice is delicious combined with white or brown rice or both. Try various proportions, but you might use half wild rice for a starter.

8. Grease the casserole or baking dish with butter or margarine before adding the ingredients to prevent sticking or burning.

9. When using in a dressing, do not pack the stuffing into the cavity of the bird or fish; rather, stuff lightly.

10. Add a little wild rice (precooked) to broths, soups, hot dishes, and even pancakes.

11. Uncooked wild rice keeps indefinitely in an airtight, dry container.

12. Cooked wild rice and wild rice dishes may be kept a few days under refrigeration or may be frozen. Storage seems to actually improve the flavor.

13. When reheating wild rice dishes, stir in enough warm water to restore the original consistency. Before serving, stir in a little butter.

14. Sour cream or yogurt enhances most wild rice recipes.

15. After cooking wild rice, pour off excess water, return to heat a minute or two to steam, fluffing with a fork to prevent burning.

III
BASIC PREPARATION RECIPES

Since nearly all recipes call for precooked wild rice, it is important that you develop your own, favorite method of preparation. With experience, the appearance of the rice will tell you when it is done; in the meantime, rely on taste. The kernels should not be hard, neither should they be mushy. If the rice is to be used in a recipe which calls for further cooking, it is better that it be a little undercooked.

In each recipe, it is important that the rice be washed thoroughly before cooking. A large sieve or colander works well.

One cup of wild rice yields about three cups of cooked rice.

METHOD #1
1. For most recipes, wash 1 cup wild rice.
2. About eight hours before you serve it or use it in another recipe, place the rice in a saucepan or kettle and cover it with about 1 quart of boiling water.
3. About 30 minutes before serving or using in another recipe, drain and rinse.
4. Cover with hot tap water, add 2 teaspoons of salt, and let simmer until done.
5. Drain and fluff with a fork, adding salt and pepper to taste. If served as a side dish, add a pat of butter to each serving.

METHOD #2
1. Wash 1 cup rice.
2. Place in a saucepan or kettle and cover with 1 quart of water.
3. Add two level teaspoons salt.
4. Bring to a boil.
5. Turn heat down, cover, and let simmer until the rice is well "flowered".

6. Fluff with a fork; let simmer a few more minutes until done to taste.
7. Drain; add butter, salt and pepper; fluff once more.

METHOD #3
1. Wash one cup wild rice; drain.
2. Place in saucepan or kettle, cover with water, and let stand over night.
3. About 45 minutes before serving time (or using in another recipe), drain and cover with 1 quart boiling water.
4. Add 2 level teaspoons salt.
5. Heat until it starts to boil again, then lower heat and let simmer, covered, for about 40 minutes or until rice is done to your taste.
6. Drain, add butter, and fluff with a fork.

METHOD #4
1. Wash 1 cup wild rice.
2. Place in a saucepan and cover with 1 quart boiling water.
3. Let stand, uncovered, 20 minutes.
4. Drain and repeat three more times. The last time, add two level teaspoons of salt.
5. Drain, add butter, season to taste, and fluff with a fork.

METHOD #5
1. Wash 1 cup wild rice.
2. Place in a baking dish and cover with 1 quart of boiling water.
3. Add 1 teaspoon salt.
4. Place in a preheated oven (350°).
5. After 1 hour, fluff with a fork. Add more water if necessary.
6. Continue baking another 20 - 30 minutes or until done to taste.
7. Add a couple of pats of butter and fluff with a fork. Add salt and pepper to taste.

IV
SIDE DISH RECIPES

6 WILD RICE WITH MUSHROOMS
1 cup uncooked wild rice
1/2 stick butter (1/8 pound)
1/2 cup mushroom stems and pieces (either canned or uncooked)
salt and pepper to taste

Cook the wild rice by any of the basic recipes listed in Chapter III, adding salt as directed.

When using uncooked mushrooms, add during last 30 minutes of cooking.

If using canned mushrooms, drain and add mushrooms during last few minutes of cooking.

When rice is done, shave butter stick into thin pats and stir in with fork as you fluff rice.

Add a little pepper and additional salt, if necessary, to taste.

If gravy is served with the meal, spoon a little over each serving.

7 WILD RICE WITH CREAM OF MUSHROOM SOUP
1 cup uncooked wild rice
1 can mushroom soup
1 small onion, chopped
1 cup celery, chopped
1 2 oz. can mushroom stems and pieces
1 small jar pimientos
1/2 small green pepper, chopped
1/3 cup slivered almonds or water chestnuts
salt and pepper to taste.

Prepare the wild rice by any of the basic recipes in Chapter III.

Sauté the chopped onion, celery, and green pepper a few minutes in oil or butter over low heat. Onions will appear "clear" when done.

Place the cooked rice in a greased casserole dish. Season lightly with salt and pepper. If salt was used in the basic preparation, be careful about adding too much.

Add the mushroom soup plus one can of water. Use the soup can to measure.

Add the celery, onions, green pepper, mushrooms, almonds, and pimientos. Stir together until thoroughly blended.

Bake in 300° oven, covered, for 1½ hours. Check occasionally for dryness. Add water if necessary.

Serve as a vegetable or side dish.

8 NUTTY RICE

1/2 cup uncooked wild rice
1 can chicken broth or chicken soup
1 small onion, chopped
1/2 cup celery, chopped
1/2 cup chopped nuts - *not* fine. Almonds, walnuts, hazlenuts, or cashews all work well—or even combinations.
your favorite seasonings

Wash rice.

Cover rice with two cups hot water and let stand overnight or about 8 hours before using. About 1 hour before serving time, drain and cover with chicken broth or soup plus two cans of water—using the can to measure. Bring to a boil, then reduce heat and let simmer for 30 minutes or until rice is well flowered (Better undercooked than overcooked at this point).

Meanwhile, sauté the onions and celery a few minutes or until the onion is clear.

Drain any excess liquid from the rice.

Please in a greased baking dish. Add onion, celery, and nuts. Lightly season with salt and pepper or your favorite seasonings, such as rosemary, thyme, parsley flakes, or marjoram. Stir together thoroughly.

Place covered dish in preheated oven (325°) for 20 minutes, fluffing with a fork once or twice in the progress.

9 SEASONED RICE IN A SKILLET

1 cup uncooked wild rice
1 can consommé or other spicy soup or broth
1 T chopped parsley
1 small onion, chopped
1 T marjoram

1 T thyme
1/2 cup celery, chopped
1/2 stick butter (1/8 pound)
salt and pepper to taste

Soak rice overnight in salted water. About 1 hour before serving time, drain and place in cast iron skillet. Cover with consommé and two cans of water, using the soup can to measure. Bring to a boil and then reduce heat, letting it simmer for 30 minutes or until rice is nearly done (kernels are mostly flowered but still a little hard).

Add onion, celery, and seasonings. Let simmer another 15 minutes or until done to taste.

Pour off any surplus liquid. Return to low heat; cut butter stick into thin shavings and gently stir into the rice, fluffing with a fork until the butter has melted.

10 BACON FLAVORED WILD RICE

1 cup wild rice
8 slices bacon, cut into narrow strips (about 1/2 inch wide)
1 onion, chopped.
1/2 cup celery, chopped
1/8 pound butter (1/2 stick)
1/2 t garlic salt
salt and pepper to taste

Prepare rice by any of the basic methods in Chapter III.

Fry the bacon strips until done, but not so crisp they are burned.

Sauté the onions and celery in butter over low heat until onions are clear.

Add bacon plus 1/2 the drippings plus all other ingredients to the hot cooked rice.

Stir together thoroughly and serve.

11 SPICY WILD RICE WITH MUSHROOMS

1 cup wild rice
2 cans chicken broth, beef broth, or consommé
1 can mushroom buttons (4 oz.)
1/2 onion, chopped
1/2 cup celery, chopped
1 T parsley, chopped (or flakes)
2 T chives, chopped
2 T green pepper, chopped
1 t oregano
1/8 # butter
salt and pepper to taste

Prepare the wild rice by any of the basic methods in Chapter III, but substitute the two cans of broth for part of the water.

Sauté the onion, celery, and green pepper in butter over low heat until onion is clear.

Drain rice if necessary.

Pour onion-green pepper-celery-butter mixture over rice.

Add mushrooms (drained), chives, and parsley and return to low heat for 15 minutes. Season with oregano and salt and pepper to taste.

12 BAKED WILD RICE WITH OLIVES AND CHEESE

1 cup wild rice
1 cup ripe olives, sliced
1½ cups mild cheese, chopped fine
1 #2 can tomatoes
1 medium onion, sliced
    (Break slices into rings or pieces of rings)
1/2 cup slivered almonds
season to taste

Prepare the wild rice by any of the basic recipes in Chapter III.

Drain if necessary.

Place in casserole; add other ingredients. Stir together. Cover casserole and bake in 300° oven for 1½ hours. Check occasionally for dryness. Add water if necessary.

13 ONION SOUP MIX - WILD RICE SIDE DISH[1]

1 cup wild rice
1 can cream of mushroom scup
1 can golden mushroom soup
1 pkg. onion soup mix
1 pint half & half cream

Pour boiling water over rice and let stand overnight. Steam rice for about 1 hour. Drain and wash.

Combine all ingredients, mix well. Bake in 350° oven for at least 1 hour. Fluff often. If too dry, add light cream.

[1]Courtesy Avis Sandland, Clearbrook, MN.

V
WILD RICE WITH VEGETABLES

14 WILD RICE AND ZUCCHINI
    1 cup wild rice
    1/2 pound zucchini slices
    1 small green pepper, chopped
    1 cup celery, chopped
    1 onion, sliced thin
    2 cans golden mushroom soup
    1 T Worcestershire sauce
    1 can tomatoes (#2 size)
    1/8 pound butter
    season to taste

Prepare the wild rice by any of the basic recipes in Chapter III.

Drain if necessary.

Sauté onions, green pepper, and celery in butter over low heat.

Place rice in greased baking dish. Add all ingredients, including sauté butter, to the rice. Stir together gently but thoroughly. Season lightly with salt and pepper.

Bake, covered, two hours in a medium oven (325 - 350°)

15 WILD RICE AND BROCCOLI
    1 cup wild rice
    1/2 pound broccoli (frozen works well)
    1 can golden mushroom soup
    1 cup mild cheese, grated
    1 small onion, chopped
    1/8 pound butter
    salt and pepper to taste

Prepare wild rice by any of the basic recipes in Chapter III.

Sauté the celery and onion in butter over low heat until the onion is clear.

Drain rice, if necessary, and place in a greased baking dish.

Add all ingredients except cheese, stir together thoroughly, and season lightly with salt and pepper.

Sprinkle grated cheese over mixture and bake in medium oven for about 30 minutes or until the cheese is melted.

Cut into squares and serve with a spatula.

STUFFING RECIPES FOR BAKED PEPPERS, SQUASH, OR TOMATOES

In each case, scoop out the seeds and membranes of the vegetable to be used. Stuff loosely and bake in a medium oven until the vegetable is tender. This will vary from less than 30 minutes for peppers and tomatoes (depending on the size) to more than an hour for squash.

A novel way of preparing squash is to cut off the top as you would a pumpkin in making a jack-o-lantern. Save the top and place it back on the squash after scooping out the seeds and ladling in the stuffing.

Peppers and tomatoes are ideal for individual servings. In the case of squash, remove the stuffing and place it in a serving dish. The squash may then be cut into serving size pieces or scooped out and served in a separate dish.

16   ORANGE FLAVORED STUFFING

3/4 cup rice
1/8 pound butter
2 T orange peel, grated
1/2 cup celery, chopped
1/2 cup green pepper, chopped
1/4 cup walnuts, chopped
juice of 1 orange
1/2 cup seasoned bread crumbs
1 T melted butter
salt and pepper to taste

Prepare the rice by any of the basic methods described in Chapter III.

Sauté the celery and green pepper a few minutes in the butter.

Mix together all the ingredients, including the butter used to sauté the celery and green pepper. Season to taste.

Ladle the stuffing into the vegetable of your choice. Hollowed out oranges also work very well with this recipe. Stir the melted butter and seasoned bread crumbs together and sprinkle them on top. Bake in medium oven (350°) until the vegetable is tender. If you use oranges, 30 minutes should be sufficient.

17 BROCCOLI STUFFING
3/4 cup wild rice
1 can cream of celery soup
1 pkg. precooked, frozen broccoli
1 cup green or sweet red pepper, chopped
1 large onion, chopped
1 cup celery, chopped
1/8 pound butter
1 medium jar pimiento (4 oz.)
salt and pepper to taste

Prepare the wild rice by any of the basic methods in Chapter III.

Thaw broccoli and cut into bite-size chunks.

Sauté the chopped onion, celery, and green pepper in butter over low heat for a few minutes or until the onions are "clear". Stir regularly so as not to burn.

Remove from heat. Add all other ingredients and stir together. Stuff lightly into the vegetable of your choice and bake in a medium oven (350°) until the vegetable is tender.

18 SPANISH STUFFING
3/4 cup wild rice
1 #2 can tomatoes
1 medium onion, chopped
1 medium green pepper, chopped
1/2 cup celery, chopped
1 small jar pimiento (2 oz.)
1 pound hamburger
cooking oil
season and pepper to taste

Prepare the rice according to any of the basic recipes in Chapter III.

Brown the hamburger in oil. Add the celery, green pepper, and onion immediately (before the hamburger starts to brown).

When hamburger is brown (stir regularly so as not to burn), add tomatoes and pimiento. Continue heating for 15 minutes; stir occasionally.

Pour over wild rice and stir together. Season to taste.

Stuff vegetable and bake until vegetable is tender.

19 Stove Top Wild Rice and Garden Vegetables
3/4 cup wild rice
6 slices bacon, cut into thin slices
1 large green pepper, cut into thin strips about 1" long
1 large onion, sliced thin
1 eggplant, skinned and cut into chunks (about 4 cups)
1 medium zucchini, sliced thin (about 1/4 to 1/3 inch)
2 tomatoes, medium. Remove seeds and slice into wedges.
1 t oregano
1 t marjoram
1 t basil
season to taste with garlic salt and pepper

Prepare the wild rice by any of the basic methods in Chapter III.

Fry the bacon strips until they begin to crispen (Do not over-fry.)

Remove bacon, reduce heat, add onion. After 3 minutes, add zucchini, green pepper, and egg plant. When zucchini and egg-plant start to brown, add tomatoes and seasonings (except garlic salt and pepper). Cover and continue over low heat for about 15 minutes, stirring occasionally.

Pour off any excess bacon grease. Add rice and stir together. Season with garlic salt and pepper to taste. Continue cooking another 10 or 15 minutes over low heat.

20 PEPPER BOATS WITH WILD RICE STUFFING[1]
1 cup wild rice
3 large green peppers
1 pound ground beef (ground round)
1/4 cup raisins
1/2 cup onions, chopped
1/2 cup carrots, chopped
1/2 cup celery, chopped
2 T slivered almonds
1/2 cup plain yogurt
1/2 cup seasoned dry bread crumbs
1 T butter, melted
1/4 t salt

Prepare the wild rice according to any of the basic recipes in Chapter III.

Remove the tops, seeds, and membranes of the green peppers and halve lengthwise, thus making 6 boats from the 3 peppers. Cook in salted water 5 minutes, drain.

---

[1]Courtesy Avis Sandland, Clearbrook, MN

Meanwhile, soak the raisins in hot water for 10-15 minutes.

In a skillet, using a little oil, combine the ground beef, onion, celery, carrots, and salt. Cook until the meat is done and the vegetables are tender; drain.

Add the wild rice (cooked), almonds, yogurt, and raisins; toss well.

Heap the mixture into the pepper boats. Place in a shallow baking dish. (12"x18"x2").

Combine crumbs and butter and sprinkle over the stuffed boats. Bake at 350° for 30-35 minutes.

21 WILD RICE WITH ASPARAGUS

3/4 cup wild rice
1 pkg. frozen asparagus (precooked)
1 can cream of asparagus soup (or cream of celery)
1 cup mild cheese (grated)
1/2 cup seasoned bread crumbs
1 T melted butter
salt and pepper to taste

Prepare the wild rice by any of the basic methods in Chapter III.

Thaw asparagus and cut bite-size. (You may substitute two cups cooked asparagus from your garden.)

Mix rice, asparagus, soup, celery, and cheese. Season to taste.

Place in baking dish. Stir melted butter into bread crumbs and sprinkle on top. Bake, uncovered, in medium oven (350°) for 45 minutes.

22 WILD RICE WITH SPINACH

3/4 cup wild rice
4 eggs, hard boiled
2 pkgs. frozen spinach
1/2 cup bacon pieces, fried but not too crisp
1 cup mild cheese, grated
salt and pepper to taste

Prepare the wild rice by any of the basic methods in Chapter III.

Meanwhile, thaw spinach. If it is not precooked, cook and drain according to directions on the package. If using fresh spinach, cook (in water) until leaves are wilted. Fry bacon pieces. Boil eggs. Shell eggs and chop (not too fine).

Prepare a white sauce by your favorite recipe or try this one:

2 T butter
2 T flour

1 cup milk
a little salt and pepper

Melt butter over low heat to prevent burning. Stir in flour and continue to cook for 3 minutes, stirring continuously.

Remove from heat and slowly stir in cup of milk. Return pan to stove and bring to a boil, stirring all the while.

Place mixture in a double boiler, add salt and pepper, and cook until sauce thickens. Beat with an egg beater.

Mix together the rice, spinach, eggs, and bacon. Salt and pepper to taste. For a little more zest, add a teaspoon Worcestershire sauce.

Carefully fold in the white sauce.

Transfer to a greased baking dish. Sprinkle the grated cheese on top. Place in a medium oven (350°) and bake, uncovered, until the cheese melts.

23   ORIENTAL VEGETABLES AND WILD RICE

1 cup wild rice
2 #2 cans oriental vegetables or 1 can each of bean sprouts, water chestnuts, mushrooms, or other chinese vegetables such as bamboo shoots.
1 pkg. frozen pea pods
1/2 cup celery, chopped
1/4 cup onions, chopped
1/8 pound butter
sweet and sour sauce

Prepare the wild rice by any of the basic recipes in Chapter III. (You may prefer a blend of white and/or brown rice with the wild rice.)

Sauté the chopped onions and celery in butter for a few minutes until the onions are clear.

Prepare a sweet and sour sauce as follows:

3/4 cup sugar
1/2 cup rice wine or cider vinegar
1/2 cup catsup
1/2 cup water
1 t soy sauce
1/4 cup corn starch

Combine sugar, vinegar, catsup, water, and lemon juice in a sauce pan. Cook over medium heat 3 to 4 minutes. Stir in soy sauce. Dissolve corn starch in 1/2 cup water; add to pan. Bring to a boil, stirring constantly. Cook until thick and clear.

Thaw pea pods, add to oriental vegetables and other ingredients and heat. Pour heated sweet and sour sauce over hot vegetable mixture and stir together. Serve hot cooked wild rice in a bowl and oriental vegetables in a separate serving dish, letting each guest spoon the sauce and vegetable mixture over the rice on his plate. You may prefer to serve the vegetables and sweet and sour sauce separately.

VI
SOUPS, BROTHS, STEWS, AND MULLIGANS

24 VEGETABLE BEEF SOUP WITH WILD RICE

5 to 6 pounds soup bone (shank with about 1 to 2 pounds meat on the bone)
2 large onions, sliced
3 large carrots, sliced
2 cups celery, chopped
1/2 cup parsley, chopped
3 large potatoes, cubed
1 #2 can tomatoes
1/2 cup uncooked wild rice, well washed
1/3 cup catsup
2 bay leaves
1 T Beau Monde seasoning
salt and pepper to taste

Using a large soup kettle, cover soup bone with one gallon water. Add seasonings and let simmer 1 hour. Add all other ingredients and let simmer 3 more hours.

Cut meat from bone and into bite-size chunks. Return meat to soup kettle or place in bowls of soup as served.

Excellent reheated.

25 SCOTCH BROTH WITH VENISON

2 pounds venison roast or stew meat, cubed into bite-size chunks
2 onions, sliced
2 carrots, sliced
2 T parsley, chopped
2 potatoes, cubed

1/2 cup wild rice, uncooked
1 bay leaf
8 peppercorns
salt and pepper to taste

Cover cubed meat with 2 quarts of water, bring to boil, then let simmer one hour. Add all other ingredients. Cover and let simmer 3 additional hours over low heat.

26 WASH DAY SOUP

2 pounds stew meat, cubed (beef, ham, or big game)
1/2 cup wild rice, uncooked
1/2 cup split peas
1 large carrot, sliced
1 large potato, cubed
1 large onion, sliced
1 large turnip, sliced
1 cup celery, chopped
1 cup cabbage, shredded or cut (not too fine)
1 bay leaf
salt and pepper to taste

Using large soup kettle, cover meat with 3 quarts of water. If you suspect meat may be tough, let simmer one hour with seasonings before adding other ingredients.

Add all ingredients except cabbage and let simmer 3 hours. Add cabbage during last 30-40 minutes.

27 PHEASANT - RICE SOUP

When preparing a dinner of pheasant or other fowl, save the necks, wings, and backs.

Prepare these parts by covering with water and adding:

1 large onion, chopped
6 peppercorns
1 bay leaf
1 t salt

Bring to a boil and cook until meat separates easily from the bones. Pick meat from the bones, discard bones, and return meat to the broth, skim.

Now add the following:

1 carrot, sliced thin
3/4 cup wild rice, uncooked
3 chicken bouillon cubes

Simmer 3 hours.

28   SMALL GAME MULLIGAN

Use whatever small game is available—squirrel, rabbit, partridge, pheasant, duck, etc. Don't hesitate to mix the game; the greater the variety the better.

Cut meat from the bone. Cut into bite-size chunks. Dredge in seasoned flour and brown in oil.

Cover with water, season with salt and pepper, and simmer 1 hour.

Then add the following:

   1 #2 can tomatoes
   1/2 cup wild rice, uncooked
   1/2 cup catsup or two cans tomato soup (or some of each)
   1 large onion, sliced
   2 beef bouillon cubes (If no poultry meat is used, use 4
       cubes and no chicken bouillon)
   2 chicken bouillon cubes (if no red meat is used, use 4
       cubes and no beef bouillon)
   2 large carrots, sliced
   1 turnip, sliced
   3 large potatoes, cubed
   1/2 cup celery, chopped
   2 T parsley, chopped

Let simmer 3 hours. Pour off liquid or add water for desired "thickness".

29   QUICK BIG GAME STEW

2 pounds roast (domestic meats or wild big game) Bake until tender, then cut into bite-size chunks.

Prepare 1/2 cup wild rice according to any of the basic recipes in Chapter III.

In a large kettle, place:

   3 cans vegetable beef stew
   1 #2 can tomatoes
   1 can mixed vegetables
   2 small cans cream of tomato soup
   the cooked wild rice

Add the meat chunks and heat (about 30 minutes on a medium burner).

30   WILD RICE AND CANNED SOUPS

This is also a good way to use up leftover wild rice dishes.

Add cooked wild rice to such canned soups as vegetable, chicken, turkey, beef, or minestrone. Add 1/2 cup cooked rice or rice leftovers to each can of soup plus 1½ cans of water.

Heat thoroughly and serve.

31 WILD RICE AND PACKAGED SOUPS

Combine:

    1 cup cooked wild rice
    1 pkg. noodle soup mix (or most any other variety)
    1 can consommé soup
    3 cups water

Bring to a boil, reduce heat, and let simmer 30 minutes.

32 "BARGAIN" WILD RICE WITH SOUPS OR STEWS

Broken wild rice kernels are usually available at a reduced price. Use this cheaper rice for "doctoring" soups and stews. Merely add 1/4 to 1/2 cup cooked rice to your favorite "from scratch" recipe for soup or stew.

Broken kernels also work just fine with either of the above two recipes (#30 and #31).

33 WILD RICE AS A SUBSTITUTE

When barley, oatmeal, or white or brown rice are called for in your favorite recipes, substitute wild rice for part or all of these ingredients.

34 CREAMY MUSHROOM WILD RICE SOUP

    1/3 cup wild rice
    2 cans cream of mushroom soup
    1/4 pound fresh mushrooms, sliced (or 1-2 oz. can)
    1/2 cup celery, chopped
    1 can chicken broth or 2 chicken bouillon cubes and
      1 cup hot water
    1 carrot, sliced thin
    2 cups half and half
    1/4 pound bacon bits, fried but not crisp
    1 t salt
    pepper (to taste)
    1/8 pound butter

Prepare the wild rice by any of the basic recipes in Chapter III.

Fry the bacon pieces, but not crisp.

Sauté the onion and celery in the butter a few minutes or until onion is clear.

Combine all ingredients in a soup pot, bring to a low boil, reduce heat, and let simmer 1 hour.

Garnish with parsley when served.

35 QUICK VEGETABLE STEW

Use left over meats or poultry or precook the meat of your choice (about one pound).

Cook 1/2 cup wild rice according to any of the basic recipes in Chapter III.

Meanwhile, sauté 1 large onion, chopped, in butter over low heat for about 3 or 4 minutes.

Place the cooked meat, wild rice, and onion in a large kettle. Then add the following:

    2 cans mixed vegetables
    1 #2 can tomatoes
    1 - 4 oz. can mushrooms (parts and pieces)
    Add water to stew consistancy.
    Heat and serve.

VII
WILD RICE WITH BIG GAME OR DOMESTIC MEATS

36 WILD RICE WITH HAM CHUNKS (casserole)

1 cup wild rice
1½ pounds precooked ham, cut into bite-size chunks
1 onion, chopped·
1 small green pepper, chopped
1 cup celery, chopped
2 cans golden mushroom soup
2 T parsley, chopped
1/8 pound butter (1/2 stick)
1 can mushroom parts and pieces (2 oz.)
salt and pepper to taste

Prepare the wild rice according to any of the basic recipes in Chapter III.

Sauté the onion, celery, and green pepper in butter a few minutes over low heat.

Chop the mushroom parts and pieces (not too small).

Place the rice in a greased casserole. Add all other ingredients and season to taste. Go easy on the salt because of the ham.

Bake in a medium over (350°) 1 hour.

37 CABBAGE ROLLS WITH WILD RICE

1/2 cup wild rice
1 onion, chopped
1 medium size head of cabbage
1½ pounds ground beef
1½ cups tomato juice
1 T Worcestershire sauce
1 cup sour cream
salt and pepper

Prepare the wild rice by any of the basic recipes in Chapter III.

Wash the cabbage. Take out the center core using a knife. Place the cabbage in hot water until the leaves tend to loosen and become limp. Carefully separate out a dozen of the larger leaves.

Mix together the hamburger, wild rice, onion, sour cream, Worcestershire sauce, and season lightly with salt and pepper.

Place about a third of a cup of the mixture on each cabbage leaf - as far as it will go. Roll up each cabbage leaf and pin with toothpicks. Cover the bottom of a baking dish with cabbage leaves and then lay the cabbage rolls on the bed of leaves. Pour the tomato juice over the rolls and place in a 325° oven for one hour and 15 minutes. Place the rolls on a serving platter and spoon tomato juice from the baking dish over each roll.

38 CHOP SUEY CASSEROLE

1 cup wild rice
1 pound pork, cubed
1 pound veal, cubed
1 onion, chopped
1 cup celery, chopped
1 can cream of celery soup
1 can cream of chicken soup
1 can mushrooms (4 oz.)
1 can Chinese vegetables
1/2 cup slivered almonds
3 T soy sauce
1/2 cup flour
1/8 pound butter
salt and pepper

Prepare the wild rice by any of the recipes in Chapter III.

Dredge veal and pork chunks in seasoned flour and brown in oil.

Place the cooked rice in a greased casserole. Add all ingredients and mix well. Add water if dry.

Bake in a medium over (350°) for 2 hours.

39 BAKED STEAK WITH WILD RICE AND MUSHROOMS

1 cup wild rice
2 pounds round steak
1 onion, chopped
1 cup celery, chopped
1 can cream of mushroom soup

1/2 cup green pepper, chopped
1/8 pound butter
1 can mushrooms (4 oz.)

Prepare the wild rice by any of the basic recipes in Chapter III.

Cut steaks into individual serving sizes. Brown in a hot skillet.

Sauté onion, celery, and green pepper in butter over low heat until onions are clear (3 or 4 minutes).

Use a greased, covered baking dish. Place all ingredients in the baking dish and mix well. Press steaks into mixture. Cover and bake 2 hours in medium oven (350°).

40 HAM LOAF

1/3 cup wild rice
1¼ pounds ham, ground coarse
1 onion, chopped fine
1/3 cup mild cheese, grated
1 cup bread crumbs
2 eggs
1/2 cup flour
salt and pepper to taste

Prepare wild rice by any of the basic recipes in Chapter III.

Mix all ingredients, thoroughly. Place in a greased loaf pan and bake 1½ hours in medium oven (350°).

Prepare a topping sauce accordingly:

1/3 cup mustard
1/3 cup crushed pineapple
1/3 cup brown sugar

Stir together thoroughly until well blended and spoon over ham loaf for last half-hour of baking.

41 PORCUPINE MEAT BALLS WITH SWEET AND SOUR SAUCE

1 cup wild rice
2 pounds ground beef
1 onion, chopped
1 small green pepper, chopped
2 eggs
salt and pepper to taste

Prepare the wild rice by any of the basic methods in Chapter III.

Mix all ingredients together thoroughly. Mold into meat balls.

Prepare a sweet and sour sauce:

3/4 cup sugar
1/2 cup catsup
1/2 cup rice wine or cider vinegar
1/2 cup water
juice of 1 lemon
1 t soy sauce
1/4 cup corn starch

Combine sugar, wine, catsup, and lemon juice in a saucepan. Cook over medium heat 3 to 4 minutes. Stir in soy sauce. Dissolve corn starch in 1/2 cup of water; add to pan. Bring to a boil, stirring constantly. Cook until thick and clear.

Place meat balls in a baking dish, pour sauce over meat balls, cover and bake 1½ hours in a medium oven (350°). Uncover last 20 minutes.

42   BAKED PORK CHOPS
1 cup wild rice
6 pork chops, thick
2 cups celery, chopped
1 onion, sliced
2 cans golden cream of mushroom soup
1 can mushrooms (4 oz.)
1/8 pound butter

Prepare wild rice by any of the basic recipes in Chapter III. Brown pork chops.

Sauté onions and celery in butter over low heat a few minutes until onions are clear.

Mix all ingredients together and with them prepare a bed for the pork chops in a greased baking dish. Place chops on top. Cover dish and bake 1 hour in a medium oven (350°). Uncover last 20 minutes.

43   HAM AND TURKEY ROLLS
1 cup wild rice
8 slices ham (each slice large enough for 1 serving)
8 slices breast of turkey or turkey roll (precooked)
1 onion, chopped
1 can cream of mushroom soup
1 can mushrooms (4 oz.) or 1 cup fresh mushrooms
1 cup sour cream
1/8 pound butter
salt and pepper

Prepare wild rice by any of the basic recipes in Chapter III. Sauté onions over low heat a few minutes until clear.

Mix (thoroughly) cooked wild rice, sour cream, mushroom soup, and onion. Season to taste.

Cover the bottom of a greased baking dish with one-half of the mixture.

Make 8 roll-ups by laying a slice of turkey on top of each slice of ham. Spoon a portion of the remaining mixture on top of the meat stacks. Form into rolls and pin with toothpicks. Lay the roll-ups on the rice bed in the baking dish and spoon the remaining mixture over each roll-up.

Bake in a medium over (350°) for 40 minutes.

44 MEATLOAF WITH WILD RICE

    3/4 cup wild rice
    1 pound ground round (beef or big game)
    1 onion, chopped
    2 eggs
    1/2 cup celery, chopped
    1 small jar pimientos (2 oz.)
    1 can mushrooms (2 oz.)
    salt and pepper

Prepare wild rice by any of the basic recipes in Chapter III.
Mix all ingredients thoroughly, and season to taste.
Place in loaf pan and bake 1½ hours in 300° oven.
Pour catsup over loaf for last 30 minutes of baking.

45 SWISS BAKED STEAK WITH WILD RICE

    1 cup wild rice
    2 pounds round steak (beef or big game)
    1 can tomatoes
    1 large can (26 oz.) tomato soup
    1 can water
    1 cup celery, chopped
    1 onion, sliced
    1 green pepper, sliced
    salt and pepper

Prepare the wild rice by any of the basic methods in Chapter III.

Cut steaks into individual servings. If you suspect steak is tough, sprinkle with flour and pound it with tenderizer hammer or butt of a table knife.

Mix together all ingredients and place in baking dish. Submerge steaks in wild rice-tomato bed.

Bake in medium oven (325°) two hours.

46   SOUTH SEAS STUFFED STEAK ROLLS

1/2 cup wild rice
2 pounds round steak
1-4 oz. can mushrooms, drained, or 1/2 pound fresh
  mushrooms
1/2 onion, chopped
1/4 pound blue cheese, crumbled
1/2 cup celery, chopped
2 T green pepper, chopped

Marinate steaks overnight, using the following recipe.

1/2 cup salad oil
2 T soy sauce
1/4 cup sugar
1/4 cup onion, chopped fine
1/8 pound butter
1/2 t salt, 1/2 t pepper
4 T sesame seeds

Cut steaks into serving size and lay flat in a shallow baking dish. Pour the marinade over the steaks and refrigerate overnight or a minimum of 8 hours. Save the marinade for basting later.

Prepare the wild rice by any of the basic recipes in Chapter III.

Sauté the onion, celery, and green pepper in the butter over low heat a few minutes or until onion is clear.

Brown steaks on each side in light oil.

Mix all ingredients together and season to taste.

Spoon the stuffing onto each steak; roll up and pin with toothpicks.

Place in baking dish. Spoon marinade over each and bake in medium oven (350°) two hours.

47   WILD RICE AND SIRLOIN[1]

2 cups rice
2 pounds sirloin steak
1 can golden mushroom soup
1 can cream of mushroom soup
1 small can mushrooms (4 oz.)
1/2 cup celery, chopped
1 cup onion, chopped
1/4 cup soy sauce
1 cup commercial sour cream

---

[1]Courtesy Mrs. Avis Sandland, Clearbrook, Mn.

1 cup half and half
1/2 cup slivered almonds (Use some in hot dish and
    balance as garnish)
2 t salt
1/4 pound butter

Prepare wild rice by any of the basic methods in Chapter III.

Cut sirloin into small chunks and sauté in butter. Add celery, onion, soups, salt, mushrooms, and sour cream, Bring to a gentle boil. Remove from heat. Add part of the almonds.

Place wild rice in a buttered 3 quart casserole. Pour the hot mixture over the rice. Toss lightly. Bake about 1 hour in 350° oven. Add some half and half if needed. Keep plenty moist and stir one or two times during baking process.

Garnish with slivered almonds.

48 VENISON AND WILD RICE HASH

1 pound ground venison
1/2 cup wild rice (makes 1½ cups cooked rice)
1 onion, chopped
1 can tomatoes
2 drops Tabasco sauce
salt and pepper to taste

Cook the wild rice by any of the methods described in Chapter III.

Brown the hamburger and onions together in a skillet (use a little cooking oil). Add the cooked wild rice to the hamburger and onions; also add the tomatoes and 2 drops of Tabasco sauce. If it appears too dry, add a little water. Stir all ingredients together as you continue to fry over low heat for about ten minutes. Season with salt and pepper to taste.

Serve with eggs.

49 WILD RICE AND HAMBURGER HOTDISH[1]

1 cup wild rice (washed)
1 lb. hamburger (beef or wild game)
1 large onion, chopped
1 cup celery, chopped
1 small green pepper, chopped
1 small jar pimientos
1 can mushroom soup
1 can water

Prepare the rice by any recipe in Chapter III.

---

[1]Courtesy Mrs. Donald Hester, Cass Lake, Minnesota

Fry the hamburger, use a little oil so it will not burn.

When it is about done, add the chopped onion, celery, and green pepper. Continue frying for another three or four minutes.

Add pimiento, soup, and water.

Mix in wild rice.

Place in a buttered casserole dish.

Bake 1-1/2 hours in a 300° oven. Add water while baking to prevent dryness.

50 WILD RICE - VENISON SAUSAGE CASSEROLE

    1½ pounds venison breakfast sausage (hamburger style) or use venison Polish sausage or other link sausage, cut into half inch chunks.

    2 large onions, chopped coarse

    3 envelopes dry chicken noodle soup mix*

    2 cups wild rice

    3 stalks celery

    1 cup slivered almonds

    1/2 t garlic powder (not salt)

    cooking oil for browning the sausage

    salt and pepper to taste

Prepare the wild rice by any of the basic recipes in Chapter III.

Brown the breakfast sausage. (If you use Polish sausage, place in saucepan; cover with water; bring to a boil; remove from heat; cover; and let set 5 minutes. Cut into chunks).

Brown the chopped onions with the breakfast sausage. If Polish sausage is used, sauté the onions in butter a few minutes over low heat. Meanwhile, prepare the chicken noodle soup in 7 cups of water, bringing it to a boil and then removing from heat.

Using a large greased casserole, stir together all ingredients, adding water if the moisture seems too dry. Bake, covered, in a 300° oven for one hour. Add water as needed to prevent dryness.

*Onion soup mix may be substituted.

51 VENISON STROGANOFF

    1/3 cup wild rice

    2 pounds venison round steak, cubed

    3 onions, sliced thin

    1 cup sour cream

    1-4 oz. can mushrooms, or 1/4-1/3 pound fresh, sliced

    1 T parsley, chopped

    1/8 pound butter

    1 T dry mustard

1 T flour
3 bay leaves
salt and pepper

Prepare wild rice by any method in Chapter III.

Sauté onion slices a few minutes in butter over low heat until clear. Remove onions and sauté venison chunks until cubes are grey on all sides. Place meat and onions in greased baking dish (with cover). Add sour cream, mushrooms, mustard, and bay leaves. Sprinkle flour over mixture, season lightly with salt and pepper, and stir together. Cover and bake in 300° oven 1 hr. and 15 minutes or until steak is tender.

Garnish with parsley and serve over hot egg noodles.

52 SPICY RICE ROLL-UP WITH HAMBURGER[1]

3/4 cup wild rice
1⅔ cups beef broth
1 cup bread crumbs
1 pound ground beef
1 egg
1/2 cup chopped green onion
1-15 oz. can tomato sauce
1 t salt
1/2 t pepper
1 cup cheddar cheese, grated
3/4 T oregano

Prepare the wild rice by any of the basic recipes in Chapter III, but use the beef broth instead of water.

Spread 1/4 cup of bread crumbs on a sheet of wax paper.

In a bowl, combine the ground beef, remaining bread crumbs, egg, onion, 1/4 of the tomato sauce, salt, pepper, and half of the cheese. Take the mixture out of the bowl and spread it in a layer on top of the bread crumbs on the wax paper.

Drain the cooked rice and spread it in an even layer on top of the meat mixture.

Roll up everything and place in a baking dish. Slide out the wax paper. Bake 30 minutes in a 350° oven.

Meanwhile, heat the remaining tomato sauce and oregano— pour over the meat roll. Top with the remaining cheese and bake another 10 minutes.

---

[1]Courtesy Mrs. Avis Sandland, Clearbrook, Mn.

53 RABBIT STEW WITH WILD RICE DUMPLINGS

1 cup cooked rice
2 small rabbits (or 1 large) cut up
1/4 cup flour
6 slices bacon
2 cups chicken broth (use soup or bouillon cubes and water)
1 can cooking onions (or 8 - 10 small stew onions)
2 cans small potatoes (or potato slices)
3 carrots, sliced
1 bay leaf
6 whole allspice
8 whole peppercorns
1 pkg. frozen peas

Fry bacon slices over medium heat until crisp. Set bacon aside and crumble. Use bacon drippings to brown rabbit parts (after dredging in flour). Place all ingredients, except carrots, in an iron kettle or deep skillet. Cook, covered, on stove top over medium heat 45 minutes (reduce heat if it boils too hard). Add carrot slices last 15 minutes. Stir occasionally.

Meanwhile, prepare wild rice dumplings according to recipe #81.

After stew has simmered for 45 minutes, drop the dumpling batter (about 8 spoons full, one at a time) on top of the bubbling stew. Cover and cook another 15 minutes (do not lift the cover during this time).

VIII
WILD RICE WITH DUCKS, UPLAND GAME, AND DOMESTIC BIRDS

54 WILD RICE AND PARTRIDGE

1 cup wild rice
1/2 cup seasoned flour
cooking oil in which to brown the partridge
1 large onion, chopped
1 green pepper, chopped
1 cup celery, chopped
1 small jar pimientos (2 oz.)
1 can cream of mushroom soup
1/8 pound butter
1 can water
salt and pepper to taste

Prepare the wild rice by any of the basic methods in Chapter III.

Cut the partridge breasts from the skeleton; dissect the wings and legs. You may also use the giblets, but to make certain they are tender, cover with water and cook over low heat 45 minutes. Cut the breasts into bite-size chunks and separate the legs into drum sticks and thighs. Roll meat in seasoned flour and brown lightly on all sides in light oil.

Sauté the onion, celery, and green pepper in the butter over low heat a few minutes or until the onion is "clear".

Place all of the ingredients in a greased casserole, season lightly, and mix well.

Bake, covered, in a 325° oven for 1½ hours. Add water from time to time if necessary to prevent dryness.

55 WILD RICE WITH DUCK CASSEROLE

1 cup wild rice
1 mallard or other large duck (or two small ducks)
1 can cream of mushroom soup
1 cup hot water
2 chicken bouillon cubes
1¼ pound fresh mushrooms, sliced
2 T grated orange peel
1 cup sour cream
1 can water chestnuts, sliced
1/2 cup green pepper, chopped
1 cup celery, chopped
1 large onion, chopped
salt and pepper to taste

Prepare the wild rice by any of the basic methods in Chapter III.

Rub the duck inside and out with salt and pepper. Roast in a low oven (225°) or crock-pot until the meat can be easily separated from the bone. Skin and pick off all meat. Cut the larger pieces into bite-size chunks. Discard skin.

Dissolve 2 chicken bouillon cubes in the cup of hot water.

Place all ingredients in a greased casserole, season lightly, and mix thoroughly. Cover and bake 1 hour in a 350° oven.

56 WILD RICE, MUSHROOMS, AND TURKEY LEFTOVERS

1 cup wild rice
2 cups turkey chunks and pieces (bite-size)
2 cups fresh mushrooms, sliced
1 large onion, chopped
1 can cream of mushroom soup
1/8 pound butter
salt and pepper to taste

Prepare the wild rice by any of the basic methods in Chapter III.

Sauté onion over low heat for a few minutes until clear. Remove with slotted spoon and add mushroom slices to the butter; sauté until tender.

Place all ingredients in a greased, covered baking dish and bake 1 hour in a 350° oven.

57 PHEASANT, PARTRIDGE, OR MALLARD WILD RICE HOT DISH[1]

1 game bird, well baked, seasoned with salt and pepper,
  basted with soy sauce, and up into bite-size
  chunks (Cornish game hen may be used)
1 cup wild rice, well washed
1 stick butter (1/4 pound)
2 cups diced celery
1 medium onion, chopped
1 large can mushroom pieces
1 can mushroom soup
4 T soy sauce (plus soy sauce for basting bird)

Prepare wild rice by any of the basic methods in Chapter III.

Roast bird, seasoned with salt and pepper, and basted with soy sauce, until well done. Cut into bite-size pieces. If desired, some breast meat may be saved and layed on top of the casserole.

In a pan, sauté the celery and onion pieces in butter. Add the meat pieces, stock from the roasting pan, drained mushrooms, mushroom soup, and 4 T soy sauce. Stir together.

Place all of the above ingredients, plus the wild rice, in a buttered baking dish—mix together well.

Dab with butter and sprinkle a little soy sauce on top. Place pieces of breast meat on top, if desired.

Bake in a 350° oven for 20-25 minutes.

Makes about 6 good size servings.

58 HALF DUCKS ON A BED OF RICE

1 cup wild rice
2 ducks, halved lengthwise
1/2 cup flour, seasoned with salt and pepper
1 can cream of mushroom soup
1 small can mushrooms (2 oz.)
1 can water chestnuts, sliced
1 cup sour cream or yogurt
1 large onion, chopped
1 cup celery, chopped
2 T green pepper, chopped
2 T grated orange peel
salt and pepper to taste

Prepare the wild rice by any of the basic methods in Chapter III.

---

[1]Courtesy Mrs. Trix Wyant, Aitkin, MN.

Halve the ducks with a stout knife or game shears.

Marinate the ducks overnight, refrigerated, breasts down, in the following solution:

3 lemons, juice of
1 large orange, juice of
2 cups cider
1/2 cup vinegar
1 medium onion, chopped
1/2 cup celery, chopped
1 t nutmeg

Roll the duck halves in flour and brown in cooking oil.

Prepare the rice bed by mixing together all ingredients. Season lightly with salt and pepper. Place all ingredients in a greased baking dish.

Lay the ducks on the rice bed, skin up. Roast uncovered in a 350° oven for 2 hours or until ducks are tender.

59 GOURMENT ROAST DUCK WITH WILD RICE STUFFING AND HONEY GLAZE OR ORANGE SAUCE

Prepare birds by scrubbing inside and out, being careful to trim away scraps of lung, etc.

Place in a large bowl, breasts down, and cover with cold water. Add two tablespoons salt per bird. Let stand in refrigerator overnight.

Prepare stuffing:

1 cup wild rice
1½ cups croutons
3/4 cup raisins
1/2 cup melted butter or margarine mixed with
    1/2 cup hot water
1 large onion
1/3 pound chopped bologna or summer sausage or
    Polish sausage or luncheon meat

Cook the wild rice according to one of the basic recipes in Chapter III.

Combine the rice, croutons, raisins, onion, and chopped meat. Season lightly with salt and pepper. Try to buy the preseasoned croutons, but if these aren't available or if you use dry bread, you may want to add a *little* sage seasoning.

Pour the melted butter-water mixture over the dressing and stir.

Take birds out of salt water, pat dry with paper towel, season with salt and pepper, inside and out.

Stuff the birds loosely. Additional stuffing may be prepared in foil; place the package alongside the bird. If there isn't room in the roaster, just set it in the oven by itself. When prepared separately, the stuffing need not be in as long as the birds—about an hour will do.

Place birds in roaster breast side up. Place a strip of fat bacon over each breast.

Add about one-half inch of water in bottom of roaster.

Cover and place in preheated low oven (250°). Bake three hours or until tender. Drumstick should wiggle easily.

Remove cover last half hour. Remove bacon strips and spread coat of honey over breasts to glaze during these last 30 minutes. Orange marmalade also forms a tasty glaze, or baste with orange sauce. *Prepared from:*

2½ tablespoons white sugar
1 cup brown sugar
1 tablespoon grated orange
1 cup orange juice (can be made from Tang or other powdered drink)
1 tablespoon cornstarch (dissolved in 1/3 cup hot water)

Combine the above ingredients and thicken in saucepan over medium-high heat; stir to prevent burning. For added zest, stir in a drop of Tabasco sauce.

60   PHEASANT BREASTS WITH WILD RICE

1 cup wild rice
4 pheasant breasts (from 2 birds)*
1 large onion, chopped
1 can golden cream of mushroom soup
1 cup sour cream
2 T green pepper, chopped
1/2 cup celery, chopped
1/8 pound butter
salt and pepper to taste

Cut breasts from carcass and marinade over night, refrigerated, in the following solution:

15 whole cloves
8 bay leaves
8 peppercorns
1 large onion, chopped
1 cup white vinegar or cooking wine
1 cup water

*Other parts of birds may be used in hot dishes, soups, or stew.

Prepare the wild rice by any of the basic recipes in Chapter III.

Sauté the onion, green pepper, and celery a few minutes in butter over low heat.

Using the same butter, lightly brown the pheasant breasts.

Mix all ingredients and place in a greased casserole.

Lay the pheasant breasts on the bed of rice, skin side up, and bake, uncovered, 1½ hours in a 350° oven.

Meanwhile, prepare a sauce from the following:

1 cup cream
2 T white wine
2 chicken bouillon cubes
1 cup hot water
2 t Worcestershire sauce

Heat sauce in a double boiler so that it will not scorch.

Serve one breast on a bed or rice on each plate. Spoon sauce over the pheasant and the rice.

61 TURKEY ROLL-UPS

3/4 cup wild rice
8 slices baked turkey or turkey roll
1 4 oz. can mushrooms
1 onion, chopped
1 cup sour cream or yogurt
1/8 pound butter
salt and pepper to taste

Prepare the wild rice by any of the basic recipes in Chapter III.

Sauté the onion in the butter over low heat a few minutes or until clear.

Prepare a white sauce as follows:

4 T butter
4 T flour
2 cup milk
4 T lemon juice
a little salt and pepper

Melt the butter over low heat (do not burn). Add flour and continue to heat for 3 minutes. Stir in the lemon juice.

Remove pan from heat and slowly stir in the milk.

Return to the stove and bring to a boil, stirring all the while.

Place mixture in a double boiler, add salt and pepper, and cook until the sauce thickens. Beat with an egg beater.

Cover the bottom of a shallow baking dish with 1/2 of the white sauce.

Mix together all of the ingredients. Spoon 1/8 of the rice mixture along an edge of each turkey slice and roll over, pinning in place with tooth picks.

Lay each roll in the baking dish with the opening down.

Spoon the remainder of the sauce over each roll-up.

Bake in a 300° oven 1 hour, uncovered.

62 DUCK BREASTS WITH WILD RICE AND ONION SOUP MIX

1 cup wild rice
3 ducks (6 breasts)
1/2 cup flour
1 pkg. dry onion soup mix
1 can golden cream of mushroom soup
2 chicken bouillon cubes
1 cup hot water
1 large can mushrooms (6 oz.)
1 small jar pimientos (2 oz.)
1 T oregano
salt and pepper to taste

Prepare the wild rice by any of the basic recipes in Chapter III.

Fillet and skin the 3 ducks, yielding 6 breasts. The legs and wings may also be used here, or the meat used in hot dishes, soup or stew.

Dredge duck pieces in seasoned flour (salt and pepper) and brown lightly in cooking oil.

Dissolve the bouillon cubes in the cup of hot water. Mix together all ingredients, seasoning lightly with salt and pepper. Lay the duck breasts on top of the rice bed. Place in a greased, covered, casserole and bake in a 350° oven for 1½ hours. Uncover the last 30 minutes.

63 CHICKEN STUFFED PEPPER BOATS

Use the recipe for stuffed pepper boats (Recipe #20).

Substitute 2 cups cubed chicken meat for the hamburger. Use chicken broth instead of water in preparing the rice.

WILD RICE DRESSING RECIPES

64 SAUSAGE STUFFING

3/4 cup wild rice
1 onion, chopped
1 cup celery, chopped

1/2 cup green pepper, chopped
1/8 pound butter to sauté onion, celery, and pepper
1/4 pound butter, melted, to add to dressing
1 cup hot water
1/4 pound sausage or chopped luncheon meats
sage to taste (go lightly if you are not sure)
salt and pepper to taste

Prepare the wild rice by any of the basic recipes in Chapter III.
Sauté the onion, celery, and green pepper over low heat (in butter) until the onion is clear.
Brown the sausage. (If luncheon meat is used, it need not precook)
Melt the 1/4 pound butter over low heat; stir in 1 cup hot water.
Combine all ingredients and stuff bird lightly.[1] Leftover stuffing may be wrapped in foil and baked alongside the bird.

65 NUTTY STUFFING

1 cup wild rice
1/2 cup chopped nuts (almonds, pecans, hazlenuts,
    walnuts, or a combination)
1 can water chestnuts, sliced
1/4 pound fresh mushrooms (or 4 oz. can)
1 onion, chopped
1/2 cup celery, chopped
1/8 pound butter
1 t sage
salt and pepper to taste

Prepare the wild rice by any of the basic recipes in Chapter III.
Sauté the onion, celery, and fresh mushrooms in butter over low heat.
Mix together all ingredients, thoroughly, as you season to taste.

66 BACON STUFFING

1 cup wild rice
8 slices bacon (thick is better)
1 onion, chopped
2 T green pepper, chopped
1 cup celery, chopped
1/8 pound butter
1 small can mushrooms (2 oz.)
salt and pepper to taste

Prepare the wild rice by any of the basic recipes in Chapter III.
Cut bacon into 1/2" strips (short way). Fry until crisp, but not burned.
Sauté onion, celery, and green pepper a few minutes in butter over low heat.
Mix together all ingredients, including 2 T bacon grease.
Season to taste.

---

[1]If you are roasting ducks or geese which are excessively fat, precook birds in a deep pot, necks down, for 45 minutes in a 400° oven. Rinse birds fat-free under the hot water tap, then stuff and bake. This avoids greasy dressing.

67 SEASONEY STUFFING

1 cup wild rice
4 cups chicken broth seasoned with 1 T Beau Monde
1 onion, chopped
1 cup celery, chopped
1/4 pound fresh mushrooms, sliced (or 4 oz. can, drained)
1/8 pound butter
1 t sage
1/4 t thyme
1/4 t oregano

Prepare the wild rice by any of the basic ingredients in Chapter III, but substitute the seasoned chicken broth for the water.

Sauté the onion and celery in butter over low heat. Remove with slotted spoon and then sauté mushroom slices.

Combine all ingredients, stirring thoroughly as seasonings are added.

68 DINNER IN A SKILLET

3/4 cup wild rice
1 pheasant (or other fowl) dissected into its parts
3 large venison (or other) sausages, cut into chunks
1 large onion, sliced thin
1 small green pepper, sliced
3 cups chicken broth (use soup or bouillon cubes and water)
1 can tomatoes (#2)
1/2 cup ripe olives, sliced
1 small clove garlic, chopped very fine
2 carrots, sliced
1 pkg. frozen peas
1 t oregano
salt and pepper to taste

Prepare the wild rice by any of the basic methods in Chapter III.

Brown sausage chunks and pheasant parts in a little oil in the skillet.* Leave drippings in skillet.

Remove meat and sauté onion and pepper slices a few minutes until onion is clear.

Place all ingredients in the pan except the carrots, cover, and cook on stove top over medium heat. After 20 minutes, add the carrot slices and continue cooking another 20 minutes or until pheasant is tender.

*A large (12" by 4" deep) skillet is required; however, a Dutch oven or iron kettle will also work well.

IX
WILD RICE
AND SEA FOOD

69 WILD RICE AND SHRIMP

1½ cups wild rice
1 pound small shrimp, cooked (at least 1 pound)
2 cups white sauce (see recipe on page 50)
1/2 cup cubed American cheese
1 onion, chopped
1/2 cup celery, chopped
2 T green pepper, chopped
1 4 oz. can mushrooms, drained
2 drops Tabasco sauce*
2 T catsup
2 T prepared horseradish
1/8 pound butter

Prepare the wild rice by any of the basic methods in Chapter III.

Prepare the white sauce by the recipe on page 50.

Sauté the onion, celery, and green pepper in butter over low heat for a few minutes or until the onion is "clear".

Mix together all ingredients—thoroughly—and place in a greased, covered oven dish and bake 1 hour at 325°.

*Alternate seasonings may be used, including 1/2 t Worcestershire sauce, 1/2 t dry mustard, 1/4 t black pepper, and 1 t lemon juice.

70 FISH LOAF

1/2 cup wild rice
1½ cups flaked fish
1/2 cup celery, chopped
1 small onion, chopped
1/8 pound butter

2 eggs
1 T parsley
1 cup half and half
salt and pepper to taste (use lemon-pepper if available or
add 2 T lemon juice to mixture.)

Prepare the wild rice by any of the basic recipes in Chapter
III.

Poach fish fillets of your choice in boiling water 10 - 12 min-
utes or until the meat flakes easily. Leftover fish (particularly
baked fish) may also be used. (The "Northern Pike into
Salmon" recipe on page 70 of "101 FAVORITE FRESH-
WATER FISH RECIPES" by this author is ideal for this loaf.)
Flake the fish from the bones until you have 1½ cups.

Sauté the onion and celery in the butter over low heat for a
few minutes until the onion is clear.

Beat the 2 eggs.

Combine all ingredients and place in a greased meat loaf pan.
Bake in a 350° oven for 1 hour.

Serve with lemon wedges; garnish with parsley.

71 WILD RICE WITH SHRIMP AND SWEET AND SOUR SAUCE

2 cups wild rice
2 pounds small shrimp, cooked
1 small onion, chopped
1/2 cup celery, chopped
1/2 cup green pepper, chopped
1 can water chestnuts, sliced
1 can Chinese vegetables (bean sprouts, etc.)
salt and pepper to taste

Prepare the wild rice by any of the basic recipes in Chapter
III.

Sauté the onion, celery, and pepper in butter over low heat a
few minutes.

Mix together all ingredients and bake in a covered, greased
dish in a 300° oven for 1 hour.

Meanwhile, prepare a sweet and sour sauce accordingly:

3/4 cup sugar
1/2 cup Chinese wine or cider vinegar
1/2 cup catsup
1/2 cup water
juice of 1 lemon
1 tsp. soy sauce
1/4 cup cornstarch dissolved in 1/4 cup water
1/4 cup frozen baby peas

Combine sugar, vinegar, catsup, water, and lemon juice in a saucepan. Cook over medium heat 3 to 4 minutes. Stir in soy sauce and dissolved cornstarch. Bring to a boil, stirring constantly. Cook until thick and clear. Stir in the peas and heat for 3 minutes.

Serve sauce separately to be spooned over each serving.

72 WILD RICE WITH KING CRAB

2 cups wild rice
1½ pound king crab, cooked
1 small onion, chopped
2 T green pepper, chopped
1/2 cup celery, chopped
1/8 pound butter
1 - 4 oz. can mushrooms, drained
1 cup sour cream
2 T lemon juice
1 t oregano
1 t thyme
salt and pepper to taste

Prepare the wild rice by any of the basic recipes in Chapter III.

Sauté the onion, celery, and green pepper in butter over low heat for a few minutes until the onion is clear.

Shell the precooked king crab and cut into 1" chunks.

Combine all ingredients, mix well as seasonings are added, and bake in a 300° oven for 1 hour or until thoroughly heated.

73 WILD RICE SALMON LOAF

1/2 cup wild rice
1½ cups flaked, precooked salmon
1/2 cup bread crumbs
1 can tomatoes
2 eggs
1/2 cup celery, chopped fine
2 T onions, chopped fine
2 T green pepper, chopped fine
1/8 pound butter
2 T parsley, chopped
2 T lemon juice
salt and pepper to taste

Prepare the wild rice by any of the basic recipes in Chapter III.

Flake the precooked salmon from the bone. Leftover baked salmon works well or else poached fresh salmon. Canned salmon may also be used.

Sauté the onion, green pepper, and celery in butter over low heat a few minutes.

Beat the eggs.

Combine all ingredients, mix well, and place in a greased meat loaf pan. Bake in a 350° oven 1 hour.

74 WILD RICE AND BAKED OYSTERS

3/4 cup wild rice
1½ cups fresh oysters
1/4 pound butter, melted
1/2 cup celery, chopped
1 can cream of celery soup
2½ cups soda cracker crumbs

Prepare the wild rice by any of the basic methods in Chapter III.

Sauté the celery in butter over low heat a few minutes or until a light brown.

Melt the 1/4 pound butter and combine with cracker crumbs.

Dilute the cream of celery soup with a can of hot water. Stir in the chopped celery.

Cover the bottom of a greased baking dish with one-half of the buttered crumbs. Add a layer of wild rice (about half of the amount prepared).

Arrange the oysters on the bed or rice.

Cover with the balance of the rice.

Pour the celery soup mix evenly over the contents of the baking dish.

Top with the balance of the buttered crumbs.

Cover, and bake in a 300° oven for 1 hour, uncover the last 30 minutes.

75 OYSTER DRESSING

1 cup chopped oysters (not too fine)
2 cups cooked wild rice
1 medium onion, chopped
1/2 cup celery, chopped
1/8 pound butter (to sauté onion and celery)
1/4 pound butter, melted
3/4 cup hot water

Sauté the onion and celery in butter over low heat a few minutes.

Combine all ingredients and stuff fish or game.

76 LEMON RUBBED AND WINE-BASTED BAKED FISH WITH WILD RICE DRESSING

Choose a large northern pike, muskie, salmon, lake trout, or whitefish. Scale* and draw the fish. Remove head, tail, and fins; wash thoroughly inside and out and dry.

Strain the juice of three lemons; salt lightly. Rub the inside and the outside of the fish—thoroughly—with the salted lemon juice. Refrigerate the fish for two or three hours.

Prepare stuffing:

1 cup wild rice
1/2 cup melted butter or margarine mixed with 1/2 cup
   hot water
1 large onion, chopped
1/3 pound chopped balogna, summer sausage, or polish
   sausage or luncheon meat
1 cup celery, chopped
1 small green pepper (or 1/3 cup)

Cook wild rice by any of the methods in Chapter III.

Sauté the celery and onions in butter for about three minutes or until the onions are translucent and the celery is light brown.

Combine the wild rice, onion, celery, chopped meat, and green pepper. Season lightly with salt and pepper. Pour 1/2 cup melted butter com ined with an equal amount of hot water over the mixture and stir the ingredients together—thoroughly.

Pat the chilled fish dry and stuff loosely. Leftover dressing may be baked separately in foil alongside the fish. Place a sheet of foil in the bottom of a roaster, then place the fish in the roaster (back up). Bring the foil up half way around the fish to hold in the stuffing. Place in a preheated medium oven (350°).

Melt 1/4 pound of butter and add an equal amount of white wine. Baste fish from time to time with the wine-butter mixture.

Bake until the meat flakes easily from the large end of the fish (about 15 to 20 minutes per pound).

Transfer baked fish to serving platter; garnish with parsley and serve with lemon wedges.

*Trout and salmon need not be scaled.

77 WILD RICE AND BAKED SNAPPING TURTLE

1½ cups wild rice
2 pounds snapping turtle meat - deboned
2 cans cream of mushroom soup
1/4 pound fresh mushrooms, sliced (or 4 oz. can)
1 onion, chopped
1/2 cup celery, chopped

1/2 cup slivered almonds
salt and pepper to taste

Clean the snapping turtle as follows:*
Both the claws and the head are "lethal", and should be removed before operating. Begin by chopping off the head. Let the turtle lie for a couple of hours because the nervous system will react at least that long after the head is removed. The "dying" process can be speeded up by boiling the turtle for a half hour; this will also make it easier to clean. Now chop off the claws. The first few times the turtle will be easier to handle if you lay him on his back on a board or old table and drive a nail through each "paw".

The next step is to remove the bottom shell. Locate the soft cartilage "crack" where the upper and lower shells are joined on each side; this may be cut with a knife. Cut away any skin that holds the lower shell. After removing the lower shell, skin the legs and remove them—including the thighs. Next, remove the meat around the neck and at the base of the shell (tail end). You will have now salvaged about 90% of the meat, so the remainder may be discarded.

Marinate the deboned turtle meat overnight in the refrigerator in the following solution:

2 T cooking oil
1 T Worcestershire sauce
1 T soy sauce
1/2 cup red wine
1/2 t salt

Prepare the wild rice by any of the basic recipes in Chapter III.

Sauté the onion and celery in butter over low heat. After a few minutes remove the celery and onions and sauté the mushroom slices until tender.

Brown turtle chunks.

Combine all ingredients (turtle meat should be cut to bite-size chunks), season to taste, and place in greased casserole. Cover and bake in a medium oven (350°) for 2 hours. Add water if mixture becomes too dry.

*Taken from *Nature's Bounty For Your Table* by this author,
Nordell Publications, Staples, MN 56479

X
WILD RICE IN BAKED GOODS

78 WILD RICE BREAD[1]

1/2 cup wild rice
1 pkg. dry yeast
1/4 cup warm water
1/4 cup brown sugar
1/2 cup molasses
1/4 cup butter, softened
2½ cups boiled - cooled water
1 T salt
1/2 cup potato buds
7 to 8 cups all purpose flour

Prepare wild rice by any of the basic methods in Chapter III.
Dissolve the yeast in the quarter cup warm water.

Using a warm bowl, add the 2½ cups of cooled water, the
yeast mixture, brown sugar, molasses, salt, butter, potato buds,
and 2 cups of flour. Beat until smooth.

Add the cooked rice (drained) and balance of flour to make a
soft dough.

Turn onto a floured board and knead for ten minutes.

Place in a greased bowl, cover, and let rise in a warm place
until about double the original volume (about 2 hours).

Divide into 4 parts and form into loaves. Place in greased
bread pans.

Cover again and let rise until almost double in bulk.

Bake 30 to 35 minutes in a 350° oven.

Cool on wire rack.

Especially good served with cheese whip and olives.

---

[1]Courtesy Avis Sandland, Clearbrook, Mn.

79 BLUEBERRY AND WILD RICE MUFFINS

1/4 cup wild rice
1/2 cup blueberries
1½ cups all purpose flour
1 cup milk
2 T sugar
1 egg
1 t baking powder
3 T soft shortening
2 T honey
2 t salt

Prepare the wild rice by any of the basic methods in Chapter III.
Sift the dry ingredients.
Beat together the egg, milk, and shortning.
Mix together all of the ingredients and spoon into greased muffin tins. (12)
Bake in hot oven (400⁰) 15-20 minutes or until muffins are golden.

80 WILD RICE AND RED RIVER CEREAL BREAD

3/4 cup wild rice flour
    (may be made in blender; use puree position)
5 cups flour
2 cups Red River cereal (available mostly in Canada)
2 pkgs. dry yeast
3 T softened shortening
1/3 cup molasses
2 t salt
1/4 cup brown sugar

Prepare cereal according to directions on the package.
Dissolve yeast.
Place cereal, wild rice flour, 2 cups white flour, salt, brown sugar, shortening, and molasses in large bowl; mix well.
Let sit a few minutes, then knead in remainder of the white flour a cup at a time—until smooth. Place in greased bowl and cover.
Let rise in warm place until about double in volume. Knead air out. Divide into loaves. Place in greased bread pans.
Bake in hot oven (400°) for 30 minutes or until done.

81   BAKING POWDER BISCUITS

1 cup cooked rice
2 cups flour
3 T soft shortening
3 T baking powder
1⅓ cups milk
1 t salt

Mix together all ingredients—thoroughly—and spoon into greased muffin tins. Bake in a hot oven (400°) 12 to 15 minutes or until brown on tops.

82   WILD RICE DUMPLINGS

1/4 cup wild rice flour or 1/2 cup cooked wild rice
2 cups Bisquick
1 egg
1/2 cup milk

Blend egg into milk.
Add wild rice and Bisquick; work together thoroughly.
Cook in soups or broths. Use 1 tablespoon of mix per dumpling; dumplings that are too large sometimes are not done all the way through.

83   MISCELLANEOUS BAKING RECIPES

The flavor of almost any baked goods is enhanced by the addition of wild rice—either in flour form or precooked.

Try it with your favorite muffin, bread, nut bread, or potato pancake recipes.

Usually 1/4 pound flour or 1/2 cup cooked rice is sufficient. Remember, the purpose is only to add an exciting touch of flavor; the wild rice is really more of a seasoning.

XI
SALADS

84   SEAFOOD SALAD

    3/4 cup wild rice
    1 pkg frozen small shrimp, precooked.
      King crab, tuna, or flaked fish may be substituted.
    1/2 cup celery chopped
    2 T chopped onion
    2 T chopped green pepper
    2 T sweet pickle relish
    3/4 cup mayonnaise
    1/4 cup catsup
    salt and pepper to taste

Prepare wild rice by any of the basic methods in Chapter III. Chill.

Combine all ingredients and serve on a bed of lettuce.

For added zest blend in 1 T prepared horseradish.

85   GLORIFIED RICE

    2 cups wild rice, precooked
    2 pkgs. strawberry jello
    4 cups hot water
    1 medium can crushed pineapple
    2 cups whipped cream (or substitute)
    1 cup marshmallow bits

Prepmre jello and set until it thickens.

Beat whipped cream and jello together; stir in remaining ingredients.

Chill before serving.

Additional whipped cream may be used as a topping.

86 GARDEN SALAD

2 cups wild rice, precooked and chilled
6 green onions, chopped (stems and all)
2 beet pickles, chopped
3 eggs, hard-boiled and chopped
1 egg, hard-boiled and sliced for garnish
2 T ripe olives, sliced
2 T celery, chopped
2 T chopped green pepper

Toss together all ingredients and place individual servings on beds of garden lettuce. Serve with vinegar and oil or salad dressing, or French dressing.

87 CHICKEN SALAD

1 cup wild rice
3 cups chicken broth
2 cups cooked chicken meat, cubed
2 T chopped green pepper
2 T chopped onion
2 T chopped celery
2 eggs, hard-boiled and chopped
salt and pepper to taste
1 cup salad dressing

Prepare the wild rice by any of the basic methods in Chapter III, except use chicken broth instead of water. Chill.
Toss together all ingredients. Salt and pepper to taste.
Serve on a bed of lettuce.

88 STUFFED TOMATO SALAD

3/4 cup wild rice
6 large tomatoes
1½ cups chicken meat, cubed
2 T chopped celery
3 garden green onions, chopped, including stems
2 T chopped green pepper
1-2 oz. jar pimientos
1/2 cup slivered almonds or water chestnuts
1 cup salad dressing

Prepare the wild rice by any of the basic methods in Chapter III. Chill.
Prepare the tomatoes by placing them stem side down and cutting *almost* through 3 times with a sharp knife, making 6 wedges. Spread wedges apart (gently) making a basket for the salad.
Combine all ingredients and stuff each tomato.

89 THREE BEAN SALAD

1 #2 can green beans, drained
1 #2 can yellow beans, drained
1 can kidney beans, drained
1 cup cooked wild rice
1/2 cup green pepper, chopped
1/2 cup onion, chopped
1 cup cider vinegar
1 T Worcestershire sauce
1 t barbeque sauce
1/2 cup salad oil
3/4 cup sugar
1 t salt
1 t pepper

Drain all three cans of beans and place them in a bowl. Stir in the green pepper and onion. Mix the oil, vinegar, and all other ingredients. Pour over beans and mix well. Refrigerate in a covered dish overnight.

XII
DESSERTS

90 RICE PUDDING

1 cup wild rice
2/3 cup raisins
2/3 cup sugar
2 cups milk
2 T cinnamon
1 t vanilla

Prepare the wild rice by any of the basic methods in Chapter III.

Combine all ingredients, spoon into custard dishes, and bake 30 minutes in a medium oven.

91 WILD RICE WITH GRANOLA

2 cups cooked wild rice
1 cup granola
1/4 cup dates, chopped
1/4 cup chopped nuts
1/2 cup brown sugar
1 small bottle maraschino cherries, chopped
whipped cream for topping

Prepare the wild rice by any of the basic methods in Chapter III. Chill.

Combine all ingredients. Serve hot or cold in desert dishes. Top with whipped cream and a cherry.

92 WILD RICE WITH FRUIT

2 cups cooked wild rice, chilled
1 #2 can fruit cocktail

1 small can crushed pineapple
1 cup miniature marshmallows
2 cups whipped cream

Combine all ingredients and either stir in or top with whipped cream and a cherry.

93 WILD RICE AND WILD BERRIES

1/2 cup wild rice
1 small can crushed pineapple
1 cup raspberries or strawberries
  (wild, if you can find them)
1 cup blueberries
4 T sugar
whipped cream for topping

Prepare wild rice by any of the basic methods in Chapter III. Chill.

Combine all ingredients and serve with whipped cream topping.

94 WILD RICE CUSTARD

1 cup wild rice
1/2 cup sugar
1 cup milk
2 T ground cinnamon or nutmeg
3 egg yolks
1/2 cup raisins

Prepare the wild rice by any of the basic methods in Chapter III.

Beat egg yolks and sugar until fluffy. Add milk as you continue beating until well mixed.

Mix raisins into cooked wild rice. Mix all ingredients.

Place in buttered custard cups. Sprinkle with cinnamon or nutmeg. Bake in a medium oven for 30 minutes, or until an inserted knife comes out clean.

XIII
BREAKFASTS

95 WILD RICE AS A HOT CEREAL

Because time is so important to most families in the early morning, it is wise to precook the rice the night before (by any of the recipes in Chapter III)., Come morning, just stir in milk until it has the consistency you prefer (try 2 cups of milk to 4 cups of hot cereal) and heat—stirring occasionally to prevent burning.

Add 1 large pat of butter to each serving.

Let each person add cream and sugar to taste (try brown sugar).

Some like it cold.

An interesting variation of oatmeal may be achieved by stirring in 1 cup of cooked wild rice to 3 cups of oatmeal during the last few minutes of cooking.

HOT WILD RICE WITH RAISINS AND CINNAMON

Prepare as in recipe #95, but add 1/2 cup raisins and 2 T cinnamon. Place the cinnamon shaker on the table for those who desire more.

WILD RICE PANCAKES AND WAFFLES
96 *With Cooked Wild Rice*

If you use a prepared mix off your grocer's shelf, add 1 cup cooked wild rice to the batter for about 24 medium pancakes or 4 waffles.

97 *With Wild Rice Flour*

Wild rice flour may be purchased in specialty shops or may be made in your own blender; use the puree position.

A good rule of thumb is to add 1/2 cup wild rice flour to every 2 cups of package mix.

4 cups white flour, sifted
1/2 t baking soda
3 T sugar
1 t salt
1/2 t cream of tartar
1 cup wild rice flour or 2 cups cooked wild rice
2 eggs, beaten
1/4 pound butter
3 cups buttermilk or sour milk—or enough to give the batter
the proper consistency for cakes the thickness you prefer

Sift together all dry ingredients.

Soften the butter and work it in with your fingers (or use 3 T cooking oil).

Add the eggs and enough milk to make a batter the consistency you prefer.

Cook on a hot griddle. It will be ready when a few drops of water will "dance" on contact.

XIV
HORS D' OEUVRES

99 POPPED WILD RICE

Prepare as you would popcorn—or—simply cover the bottom
of an iron skillet with a generous layer of cooking oil (peanut oil
seems to work best). Add about 1/2 cup of wild rice if you are
using about a 10" pan. Place over medium heat, rotating the
pan occasionally. Remove popped rice with a slotted spoon and
add more uncooked rice. Serve sprinkled with a little salt and
melted butter.

100 MINI-PORCUPINES

     1 cup wild rice
     2 pounds ground beef
     1 onion, chopped
     1 small green pepper, chopped
     2 eggs
     salt and pepper to taste

Prepare the wild rice by any of the basic recipes in Chapter
III.

Mix all ingredients together thoroughly. Mold into tiny meatballs.

Place meatballs in a greased, covered baking dish and bake
1½ hours in a medium oven (350°). Uncover last 20 minutes.

Serve on toothpicks with a bowl of your favorite barbeque or
sweet and sour sauce, piping hot.

101 WILD RICE AND CHICKEN LIVER CANOPES

1 cup wild rice
10 chicken livers
1 large onion, chopped
1/8 pound butter
salt and pepper to taste

Prepare wild rice by any of the basic recipes in Chapter III.
Sauté the livers and chopped onion in butter over low heat.
Chop liver, fine.

Stir together all ingredients, including the butter used to sauté the livers and onion.

Serve hot on crackers or in mini-sandwiches.